INVITED TO KNOW GOD

THE BOOK OF DEUTERONOMY

Other titles in the Transformative Word series:

INVITED TO KNOW GOD

THE BOOK OF DEUTERONOMY

TRANSFORMATIVE WORD

A.J. CULP

Series Editors
Craig G. Bartholomew & David J. H. Beldman

LEXHAM PRESS

Invited to Know God: The Book of Deuteronomy
Transformative Word

Copyright 2019 A.J. Culp

Lexham Press, 1313 Commercial St., Bellingham, WA 98225
LexhamPress.com

Print ISBN 9781683593508
Digital ISBN 9781683593515
Library of Congress Control Number:2019949170

Series Editors: Craig G. Bartholomew and David J. H. Beldman
Lexham Editorial: Abigail Stocker, Holly Marr
Cover Design: Kristen Cork
Typesetting: Abigail Stocker

For my children:

Elijah

> A little piece of my own soul
> walking beside me in this world.

Hadassah

> Life's strongest spell
> is a little girl's love for her daddy.

TABLE OF CONTENTS

Oh to grace how great a debtor,
    daily I'm constrained to be.
Let thy goodness like a fetter,
    bind my wandering heart to thee.

"Come Thou Fount of Every Blessing"
E. Margaret Clarkson adaptation

A LENS FOR READING

I would like to begin by offering an analogy for reading this book, one that comes from Charles Dickens's *A Christmas Carol*. You will remember the story, I'm sure: Ebenezer Scrooge finds himself caught up in an unwanted adventure, being whisked around by three Christmas spirits, the ghosts of Christmas Past, Present, and Future. The Ghost of Christmas Present is the one we'll find helpful for reading Deuteronomy.

The ghost appears as a jolly giant in a green robe, a wreath of holly on his head and an empty old scabbard on his side. He sits in the midst of a grand feast and holds a torch like a cornucopia; a roaring fire fills the hearth and "living green" ivy and holly and "bright gleaming berries" grow in the room like a garden. When Scrooge peeks around the corner, the ghost calls out, "Come in and know me better, man!" The ghost then transports Scrooge around the city to witness things happening at that very moment. Scrooge finds the scenes are of two kinds: some of joy and festivity, others of want and despair.

One poignant image comes at the closing of the scene portraying the Cratchit family: "'I see a vacant seat,' replied the Ghost, 'in the poor chimney-corner, and a crutch without an owner, carefully preserved. If these shadows remain unaltered by the Future, the child will die." The idea of Tiny Tim dying confronts Scrooge and he cries out, "No, no ... Oh, no, kind Spirit! say he will be spared." But his protests are met with his own words from earlier in the day, now spoken back to him by the ghost: "If they would rather die, they had better do it, and decrease the surplus population."

Scrooge notices the ghost growing older as the night passes, and by midnight he has become gray and gaunt. Just before passing, though, the ghost presents the apparitions of two ghastly children clutching at his robes. These, he tells Scrooge, are named after humanity's failings: Ignorance and Want. The ghost warns Scrooge to beware especially of the boy, Ignorance, for written on his brow is "doom, unless it be erased." At this the ghost disappears forever.

The ghost's message thunders home: *now* is the time to act. The present is the hinge that turns the past to the future. Left unchanged, the mistakes of the past become

---

OUTLINE OF DEUTERONOMY

☐ **Deuteronomy 1–4**: Overview of Israel's life with Yahweh since the exodus

☐ **Deuteronomy 5–11:** Instructions on how Israel should live as Yahweh's people

☐ **Deuteronomy 12–26:** More specific instructions about the nature of this life

☐ **Deuteronomy 27–34**: Preparing Israel to live faithfully after Moses has died

the shackles of the future, but if action is taken, that future can be brighter. The ghost's invitation, then, to "come in and know me better, man!" is a call to choose the path of life and flourishing represented in his lavish feast, living green plants, and empty scabbard of peace. Yet the ghost's warning is real as well; the disturbing images will become reality if change is not made. Even with the ghost gone, his message still echoes: *now* is the time to act.

This little story is an apt analogy for Deuteronomy, with three elements being especially noteworthy:

1. **An invitation**: like the Ghost of Christmas Present, Yahweh—the Lord of Israel—extends an invitation: "Come in and know me better!" Indeed, at the heart of Deuteronomy is this concern with knowing God *truly*. As with Dickens's story, Deuteronomy sees such knowledge leading beyond mere piety to righteous living and ethics.

2. **A present call**: as the ghost did with Scrooge, so Deuteronomy takes its audience on a journey rehearsing the good and the bad of the past, the point of which is to drive home the need to change things *now*: "Now choose life" (Deut 30:19).

3. **Of fear and flourishing**: also like the ghost, Deuteronomy's primary invitation is to a life of goodness and flourishing. Akin to the room full of food, light, and living green, Deuteronomy portrays the possibility of abundant life in the promised land. Akin to the image of a crutch without its owner, though, the text also portrays

> the possibility of the land without Israel, the
> people destroyed, deported, and far from God.

As we come to Deuteronomy, therefore, let us keep these
three things in mind. Let us hear in it the voice of God
calling out to us: *come in and know me better*!

SUGGESTED READING

☐ Deuteronomy 4:1–40

☐ Deuteronomy 30:1–11

Reflection

Have you ever considered Scripture in this way before—
that is, as an invitation into God's presence in order to
know him better? How does this change your expectations
for Deuteronomy?

_____

_____

_____

When read as an invitation, what are the above passages
inviting us *into*? That is, what kind of an invitation is this?

_____

_____

_____

What would you say the goal of Deuteronomy's invitation is?

_____

_____

_____

2

INTRODUCING DEUTERONOMY

While we want to know God better, many of us find this difficult in the case of Deuteronomy. The book can seem like a collection of random material, from ancient travel itineraries to ancient laws, none of which appears terribly helpful for life today. As we shall see, though, the book is far from random or antiquated, for it has been crafted for the very purpose of helping each new generation encounter the living God of Scripture. It seeks to do this in two ways. Firstly, and as we've already seen, it offers an *invitation*—calling each generation to come and know God better. Secondly, it provides the *means* for making good on this invitation. The goal of *Invited to Know God* is to highlight some of these means of knowing God so that we ourselves might make good on Deuteronomy's invitation.

Deuteronomy as Sermon

The first step in understanding Deuteronomy is to correct a critical misunderstanding: it is not a book of law. Certainly the book includes law and in some respects revolves around law, but it is not a book *of* law. The book is rather about love for Yahweh, Israel's covenant Lord, who delivered Israel from slavery and bound himself in relationship to his people at Mount Sinai. In this way, Deuteronomy stands not in opposition to the gospel but as an example of it. Its logic is the very same: since God has graciously delivered you, you in turn should live in a certain way. This way of living, in Old Testament terms, begins by obeying the law. So Deuteronomy does not merely rehash the law but retells of Yahweh's goodness in order to motivate obedience to it.

A helpful analogy for what we find in Deuteronomy is the final message of a pastor who has planted a church but now, after many years leading it, learns he is dying. The pastor stands before the people one last time, hoping to provide them with his final words on how they can continue to live before God in his absence. He looks back over their long history together, highlighting God's provision and their own successes and failures. He draws on Scripture and the church's constitution, but his point is not to repeat these things. His point is to *exposit* them—to clarify their substance and motivate people to obey them in his absence. Upon finishing, the dying man presents a copy of his sermon to the elders. The hope is that the elders will keep the sermon safe as their founder's final exhortation on living life before God.

Despite its reputation, therefore, Deuteronomy is not a book of law. It's a sermon, an *exposition of the law*. God has told Moses, Israel's faithful and long-suffering leader, that he will die before entering the land. Now standing on the plains of Moab, looking over the Jordan River to the hills of Israel, Moses knows his time is short. So he delivers his swan song—his final sermon to Israel. He reiterates the nature and substance of Israel's covenant relationship with Yahweh and drives home the singular goal of the law—to learn to love the Lord.

More than a one-time event, Moses' sermon is recorded and stored for a continuing role in the life of Israel. We see a snapshot of that role in Deuteronomy 31:10-11, 24-26, where Moses commands the priests and Levites to place a copy alongside the ark of the covenant and to read it at regular intervals. The placement of the sermon along-side the ark, which contains the Ten Commandments, is a perfect illustration of Deuteronomy's role: to stand as an ongoing exposition of the covenant, calling Israel to observe its central tenet: "Hear, O Israel: The LORD our God, the LORD is one. Love the LORD your God with all your heart and with all your soul and with all your strength" (Deut 6:4-5). What each generation will therefore "hear" is the voice of Moses calling the people to love their Lord.

Deuteronomy as Treaty

There is one more important piece to hearing Deuteronomy as the voice of Moses: the form of the text. It is not obvious to our modern eyes, but Deuteronomy is shaped according to the conventions of an ancient document called a *vassal treaty*. In the ancient world, vassal treaties were forged between two parties: a more powerful party (the suzerain, or overlord) and less powerful party (the vassal, or slave). Empires often used these treaties to manage relationships with smaller people groups. The treaty itself formalized the nature of the relationship, outlining the parties' past history together and the expectations going forward.

From approximately 1600 BC to 1200 BC the Hittite empire stretched across modern-day Turkey and down into Syria. The Hittites administered their affairs through various forms of written communication, many of which were inscribed on clay tablets and kept in the archives of the cities. Today archaeologists have uncovered some 30,000 clay tablets from the capital city of Hatussa alone, and among these were treaties between the Hittites and the kingdoms under their power. These treaties are valuable because they provide a historical backdrop for understanding Deuteronomy as literature, since Deuteronomy seems to have been modeled after their form:

HITTITE TREATY	DEUTERONOMY
☐ Preamble	☐ 1:1–5
☐ Historical Overview	☐ 1:6–4:49
☐ General Stipulations	☐ 5–11
☐ Specific Stipulations	☐ 12–26
☐ Deposit of Text	☐ 1:24–26
☐ Public Reading	☐ 31:10–13
☐ Witnesses	☐ 31:19, 26, 28
☐ Blessings	☐ 28:1–14
☐ Curses	☐ 28:15–68

Deuteronomy is unique, though, in that it uses this political treaty form for religious reasons, namely to depict the relationship between Yahweh and Israel. Yahweh is portrayed as the suzerain and Israel as his vassal, and the book of Deuteronomy proceeds accordingly. Chapters 1-4 recount the history of the relationship between Yahweh and Israel. It begins in Egypt with Yahweh's deliverance of Israel and carries on right up to the present moment at Moab, as the people stand overlooking the promised land. During this historical overview, two portraits emerge: Yahweh as a good and faithful partner and Israel as a stubborn and wayward one.

In light of the history of the relationship, chapters 5-26 move to outline the general (chs. 5-11) and specific (chs. 12-26) stipulations. It is no accident that the Ten Commandments are at the head of these stipulations (ch. 5), for they serve as a constitution for the covenant people. And it is no accident that the Ten Commandments and the stipulations sections all begin with the worship of Yahweh before moving on to ethics (5:6-11; 6:4-5; 12:1-32). This shows the fundamental idea in Deuteronomy that right worship is the fountainhead for right living.

Chapters 27-28 follow on logically from the stipulations section, giving instructions for a covenant renewal ceremony upon entering the land (ch. 27) and outlining the blessings and curses attached to the covenant (ch. 28). If Israel continues to love Yahweh and obey his law, they will enjoy the blessings of a life of flourishing in the land. If Israel does not, however, they will incur the curses— human suffering, a barren land, and eventual banishment from the land. The final important piece of the treaty is the so-called document clause, which details how the treaty is to be stored and then read aloud periodically. This ensured the relationship would be kept fresh, when at regular intervals the treaty was read aloud and the people recommitted themselves to the suzerain. In Deuteronomy, we find these elements in 31:10-13, 24-26, which dictate that, at the very least, the treaty (Deuteronomy) would be read before the people every seven years.

Of these, two elements are perhaps most enlightening in regard to the relationship between Yahweh and Israel: the historical section (Deut 1–4) and the blessings (Deut 28). The reason these are enlightening is because they reveal how Yahweh sought to motivate obedience to himself. There were different treaty options in the ancient world. One option was the Assyrian style, which included neither the historical section nor the blessings—it only used threat of punishment and curses. This treaty is known for being based on fear: it used terror to motivate people's obedience. Another style of treaty was the Hittite version, which, while employing curses, more prominently featured the historical section and the blessings. As such, it is known for seeking to motivate loyalty through devotion; by reminding the people of the overlord's past benevolence and promise of future blessing, the treaty inspired the people to continue loving and trusting the overlord.

In using the historical section and the blessings, therefore, Deuteronomy indicates the relationship between Yahweh and Israel is one built on love. Time and again the book answers the question of why people should obey Yahweh, "Because he loved your ancestors and chose their descendants after them, he brought you out of Egypt by his Presence and his great strength" (Deut 4:37). In other words, the Lord has continually been good to his people and has promised them a future, and they are to love him in return. The message of Deuteronomy, then, is captured well in 1 John 4:19: "We love because he first loved us."

Goodness Like a Fetter

Yet for many of us, it is still difficult to discern God's voice speaking *to us* in Deuteronomy. After all, we do not feel particularly embraced by the idea of entering a treaty with anybody, even God, and we do not feel that by reading a treaty document we are particularly enlightened in our daily living. These are fair points, ones we shall address as this book goes on. But for now it is helpful to point out a key distinction: Deuteronomy is a covenant, not a treaty.

True, Deuteronomy employs the form and language of an ancient treaty, but not because it's a treaty itself. Rather, the book takes the political practice of *treaty making* and uses it instead for the religious purposes of *covenant making*. To say it differently, Deuteronomy's form is like a political treaty, but its substance is that of a religious covenant. This may seem incidental, but it is actually quite important, for covenants are very different from treaties.

Biblically speaking, a "covenant" (*berit*) was a formal agreement between two people or between God and people. Here we think, respectively, of Abraham and Abimelech (Gen 21:22–34) and God and Abraham (Gen 15; 17). Treaties, in contrast, were agreements between nations, such as Egypt and the Hittites. The primary difference was the realm of the relationship: treaties functioned in the political realm, covenants in the interpersonal realm.

What Deuteronomy deals in, then, is not political matters but personal ones. Yahweh's invitation to the people of Israel is in fact an extension of his commitment to persons—Abraham, Isaac, and Jacob. As such, the covenant that was initiated with Abraham and continued through to Jacob is affirmed and redefined in Deuteronomy. As we shall see, this covenantal relationship will extend further yet—through the Davidic king and into the new covenant. The new covenant, of course, is where we today find entry into this ancient relationship between God and his people. But the point remains the same: the invitation in Deuteronomy is to a *relationship* with the covenant Lord.

The question, though, is why Deuteronomy would use political language to outline a personal relationship. Doesn't such treaty language undermine the very idea of covenant with Yahweh? To be sure, we can only guess at why this might be, but I have found the ideas of scholar Peter Craigie to be quite helpful.[1] He suggests that the reason lies in Israel's former identity as slaves in Egypt. Since Israel was enslaved by Egypt and Egypt used vassal treaties, it is quite possible that the Israelites themselves were under a vassal treaty there. Pharaoh would have been the suzerain and Israel his vassal, and the demands would have been cruel and exacting. When, in the exodus, the Lord freed the people from this bondage, he would have wanted to cast the newly established relationship in terms that were familiar. Hence the vassal treaty.

Yet he also would have wanted to communicate the radical differences as well and so chose the Hittite style of treaty because it rooted the relationship in love and loyalty rather than fear and terror. Even more, it transformed a key idea—covenant—within this relationship. Craigie notes that the Egyptian term used for "covenant" carried connotations of imprisonment. At times it was even used for the implement that held a slave captive—a "shackle" or a "fetter." So when Israel's redeemer, Yahweh, used this term to define the new relationship between the people and himself, it took on new meaning. Covenant became the thing that bound Israel to their redeemer rather than their taskmaster, and it was a relationship based on love rather than fear.

Perhaps, then, we might understand the treaty-covenant through the language of the classic hymn "Come Thou Fount":

> Oh to grace how great a debtor,
>   Daily I'm constrained to be
> Let thy goodness like a fetter
>   Bind my wandering heart to thee

In Deuteronomy, as in Christianity, we are bound to our Lord. Yet the ties that bind us are not slavery and fear but freedom and love. God in his goodness has acted on our behalf, and we in turn, out of gratitude and love, choose to bind ourselves to him. And we can say with the hymnist, "Let thy goodness like a fetter bind my wandering heart to thee."

SUGGESTED READING

☐ Deuteronomy 29:1–15

☐ Deuteronomy 34:1–8

Reflection

Have you ever thought of Deuteronomy as the final sermon of a beloved pastor? How does this affect your perception of the book's message?

_____

_____

_____

_____

For you, how is it significant that Deuteronomy's aim—to invite people into covenant with God—is primarily interpersonal in nature rather than, say, legal or political?

_____

_____

_____

_____

What do you think is the significance of the fact that Deuteronomy motivates obedience primarily based on God's goodness rather than his wrath?

_____

_____

_____

_____

3

DEUTERONOMY 1–4: MEMORY AS A MEANS OF KNOWING GOD

I don't know many people who appreciate Deuteronomy 1–4. Most skip over it, if possible, when reading through the Bible, for it features everything difficult about the Old Testament: odd people and places and no apparent connection to life today. Yet as we shall see, these chapters play an important role in opening the book—they set the stage for the work as a whole. In short, they characterize the book as a spiritual travelogue, with the purpose of inviting each new audience into a journey with Yahweh.

On the Road

On the Road is a classic novel by Jack Kerouac, chronicling two friends and their wanderings across the landscape of America in the 1940s. The storyline itself seems to ramble from one location to the next, featuring a host of odd figures and revolving around drinking, drugs, and sex. For this reason, some have seen the book as a travelogue of empty pleasure seeking. But if we look a little closer, we see something more significant. The story represents the journey of the Beat Generation, a generation that had grown disenfranchised with society, feeling that the government merely used its people and that culture at large couldn't see past trivial things. As such, many of its young people rebelled against traditional norms and went searching for meaning in new ways. And while we might see debauchery in the details of *On the Road*, the sojourners themselves saw their journey as a spiritual one. Indeed, Kerouac once described *On the Road* as a tale of two "Catholic buddies roaming the country in search of God."[2] The story, though warped and knotted, is a spiritual travelogue.

Deuteronomy 1–4 is similar in some important ways. The section reads like a collection of random historical places and names: for instance, the Valley of Eshkol; Kadesh Barnea; Shechem; the Anakites; the Horites; Sihon, king of Heshbon; or Og, king of Bashan. And it recounts some of Israel's glaring indiscretions, including the cowardice of the spies, Moses being banned from the land, and the sinful tendencies of the people. Yet these are not the point of the material; the point is to create a spiritual travelogue.

A key difference between *On the Road* and Deuteronomy as travelogues is in the nature of their journeys. Kerouac's work chronicles a journey of leaving old ways in order to find meaning, but Deuteronomy does the opposite, revealing the source of present meaning as Israel's original journey with Yahweh, from Egypt to promised land. It was there that Yahweh revealed himself definitively to Israel and there that Israel's character as a people was revealed, too, and it is there that the people must return if they are to journey as God's people.

As a travelogue, therefore, Deuteronomy aims to do more than merely recount Israel's history; it aims to draw each new audience into the journey. It is a kind of enchanted travelogue whose very words are a portal to ancient times and places. The times and places in view are the key moments of Israel's journey from Egypt to promised land, when they stood before Yahweh. In this way, each new audience does not merely observe the events but participates in them.

Joining the Journey

But how can a book accomplish such a feat? It happens through something called collective memory. Collective memory is how communities address the age-old problem of helping individuals identify with the group. The problem is that in order for individuals to become part of a group, they must identify with its defining moments; the defining moments, however, are typically ones that occurred in the distant past. As such, the very events with which people need to identify are ones they have not experienced.

Enter collective memory. Through various kinds of commemoration, communities make people familiar with important events that allow them to share the community's identity. Take September 11, for instance. Very few Americans actually experienced the event, but most still would identify with it, even "remembering" the plane flying into the tower and the ash-covered people running away. The reason they remember it is because—through song, story, video, and commemorative rehearsal—they have come to see themselves as participants in the event.

Deuteronomy seeks to do something similar. It wants the people of each new generation to see themselves, in some sense, as participants in Israel's defining era—the exodus journey. We notice this if we look closely at the text itself. The book opens by distinguishing the present audience from the past generation—that is, the generation raised in the wilderness and now standing before Moses at Moab—and from the exodus generation, who died in the wilderness.

> [The LORD] solemnly swore: "No one from this evil generation shall see the good land I swore to give your ancestors." (Deut 1:34–35)

> Thirty-eight years passed from the time we left Kadesh Barnea until we crossed the Zered Valley. By then, that entire generation of fighting men had perished from the camp, as the LORD had sworn to them. The LORD's hand was against them until he had completely eliminated them from the camp. (Deut 2:14–16)

The point could not be clearer: the exodus generation is dead and gone.

Yet something curious follows: the book goes on to treat its audience as if they were the exodus generation. Consider some examples from Deuteronomy 4 (italics added):

> *You* saw with *your own eyes* what the LORD did
> at Baal Peor. The LORD your God destroyed
> from among *you* everyone who followed the
> Baal of Peor, but all of *you* who held fast
> to the LORD your God are still alive *today*.
> (vv. 3–4)

> Only be careful, and watch yourselves
> closely so that *you* do not forget the things
> *your eyes have seen.* ... Remember the day *you*
> stood before the LORD your God at Horeb.
> (vv. 9–10)

> By testings, by signs and wonders, by war,
> by a mighty hand and an outstretched arm,
> or by great and awesome deeds, like all the
> things the LORD your God did for *you* in
> Egypt before *your very eyes*? *You* were shown
> these things so that you might know that the
> LORD is God; besides him there is no other.
> From heaven he made *you* hear his voice. ...
> On earth he showed *you* his great fire, and
> *you* heard his words from out of the fire. ...
> He brought *you* out of Egypt by his Presence
> and his great strength ... to bring *you* into
> their land to give it to *you* for your inheri-
> tance, as it is *today*. (vv. 34–38)

No mere slip of the tongue, Moses repeatedly calls the
people to remember things from the exodus generation,
often with great vividness. He treats them as if they
were eyewitnesses.

What we're looking at here is a mnemonic technique that facilitates a sense of time travel. The repeated use of "you," on the one hand, makes the audience feel as if they themselves were participants in the events rather than just observers. On the other hand, the continued rehearsal of what "your eyes" saw, followed by vivid descriptions of the events, creates powerful images of the events in the audience's mind. Cumulatively, these facilitate a fusing of generations, wherein new audiences sees themselves as a kind of participant in the exodus events.

Three events—and the places where they occurred—are central to the exodus story: Mount Horeb (or Sinai), where Yahweh revealed himself and forged a covenant with Israel; Kadesh Barnea, where Israel sided with the spies and was punished with forty years of wilderness wandering; and Moab, where the next generation now stands, at the border of the promised land, with a chance for a new beginning. Deuteronomy also looks forward to two future places: Shechem—where, once in the land, Israel will celebrate their first covenant-renewal ceremony—and the "chosen place" where, once settled, Israel will annually worship Yahweh. This place is later named "Jerusalem," but Deuteronomy knows it only as the "chosen place."

Deuteronomy's point, though, is not merely to help people identify with these events but to draw them into what the events represent: a journey through "moments of decision."[3] The cornerstone of the journey is Yahweh's self-revelation to and covenant making with Israel at Mount Sinai, where Israel chose to commit to Yahweh. Yet Israel would face challenges as they tried to live out this commitment, and the events after Mount Sinai represent their success and failure in doing so. What Deuteronomy seeks to instill is not just the memory of good and bad choices but the perpetual question facing God's people: How now will you live? In the light of Yahweh's self-revelation and gracious covenant offer, will you choose to follow him or turn away? Deuteronomy's call to all people everywhere is "Now choose life" (Deut 30:19).

The problem is: how might the journey experience and the call to choose life extend to each new generation? Originally, the people received the message aurally, from the mouth of Moses as he spoke the words on the plains of Moab. Thereafter, Moses' words were captured in the book of Deuteronomy, which was to be read every seven years. But how were the words to live on in an otherwise oral, largely illiterate culture?

Deuteronomy itself outlines what we might call *conduits* of memory. These ensured that each new generation could identify with Israel's defining events and choose life with Yahweh. Four such conduits are central: daily habits, song, story, and ritual. We find instructions for daily habits in Deuteronomy 6:6–9, which exhorts parents to teach children the heart of the covenant. "Love the LORD your God with all your heart and with all your soul and with all your strength" (Deut 6:5). The text mentions a variety of practices, but the gist is that parents ought to engrain love for the Lord in children, always and everywhere. Song, too, is part of the memory program that happens in the home. In contrast to daily habits, the song (Deut 32) is sobering and mournful. It focuses on the fact of Israel's historic bent toward rebellion despite Yahweh's long-suffering faithfulness. Apparently, parents were to sing it over their children, reminding them of Yahweh's past goodness and Israel's stubborn heart.

Story also happened in the home. Realizing children would wonder about the meaning of the covenantal shape of their lives, Deuteronomy instructs parents to tell the story of Israel's deliverance from Egypt (Deut 6:20–25). The point, in particular, is to show that Yahweh's call upon their lives is not random or arbitrary but born of his past goodness. Because he was good to Israel and delivered them from bondage, the people should show their gratitude by obeying Yahweh. By telling the redemption story, therefore, each new generation joins the story and learns to love the Lord in this way. While Jewish practice has formalized this storytelling as part of the Passover feast, Deuteronomy imagines the story being retold more generally within the home. Whenever children ask about the oddity of their own lives compared to their nonbelieving neighbors, parents are to recount the story of God's goodness.

The final memory conduit, ritual, is different from the other three in that it functions in the public rather than domestic sphere. Deuteronomy 16 portrays three feasts as especially important times when all Israel would travel from their villages to gather for worship at the chosen place. While each of the three feasts—Passover/Unleavened Bread, Weeks, and Tabernacles—has its distinctives, the most important point is how they together reenact the exodus journey. Passover, at the beginning of Israel's year, commemorated the period of the exodus from Egypt into the wilderness, focusing on the experience's difficulty and affliction. The Feasts of Weeks and Tabernacles commemorated the exodus journey's movement into the land, focusing on the blessing and joy of living life in the land. The cumulative result was that over the course of the year Israel would reenact through ritual the exodus journey—traveling from the sorrow of Egypt and the wilderness to the joy of the promised land. In so doing they were, time and again, drawn into the journey to stand before Yahweh at a moment of decision.

Part of Israel's remembering happened through daily habits, or *habitus*, whereby parents taught their children the things of faith as they went about their household chores. This is reflected in Deuteronomy 6:6–9, which instructs parents to place God's words upon their hearts, to tie them to their hands and forehead, and to engrave them on their doorposts and gates. While we don't know exactly what this would have looked like, we do have some ancient practices that shed light on it. For instance, in a burial cave near Jerusalem, at a site called Ketef Hinnom, archaeologists found two tiny silver scrolls, inscribed with parts of Numbers and Deuteronomy, from around 650 BC. These were apparently worn as pendants, in life and death, as a way of keeping God's words "upon the heart" as a reminder. Also, among the Dead Sea Scrolls (c. 250 BC to AD 68) were found containers, with parts of Exodus and Deuteronomy, that were worn on the head and hands as reminders. Indeed, these are the precursors to what Jews practice today, binding Scripture to head and hands to pray (*tefillin*) and keeping it within a capsule on their doorposts (*mezuzah*).

Knowing God through Memory

But how does the call of Deuteronomy 1–4 extend to us today—not just as God's people but as Christians? The New Testament grafts us into the ancient journey through the Passover, which Christ makes a celebration of *his* death:

> While they were eating, Jesus took bread, and when he had given thanks, he broke it and gave it to his disciples, saying, "Take it; this is my body." Then he took a cup, and when he had given thanks, he gave it to them, and they all drank from it. "This is my blood of the covenant, which is poured out for many," he said to them. (Mark 14:22–24)

Most of us recognize the theological importance of this: that Christ identifies himself as the Passover lamb and his crucifixion as the sacrifice. But what we often miss is how it connects Christian worship to the ancient journey found in Deuteronomy. When Christ invites his disciples to participate in this way, he transforms the Passover into the Lord's Supper. As such, the disciples no longer participate in the ancient journey as Jews but as Christians, as those who acknowledge Christ as Messiah and Lamb of God.

Yet as the apostle Paul makes clear, the call extends beyond the twelve disciples to us today:

> For I received from the Lord what I also passed on to you: The Lord Jesus, on the night he was betrayed, took bread, and when he had given thanks, he broke it and said, "This is my body, which is for you; do this

in remembrance of me." In the same way,
after supper he took the cup, saying, "This
cup is the new covenant in my blood; do this,
whenever you drink it, in remembrance of
me." For whenever you eat this bread and
drink this cup, you proclaim the Lord's death
until he comes. (1 Cor 11:23-26)

When we partake of the Lord's Supper, therefore, we are
doing more than merely remembering. We are standing
before the Lord at a moment of decision. Here the ancient
call of Deuteronomy extends to us through Christ, who
asks not whether we will choose life *or* death but life
through death. There we behold our crucified Lord, who
bids us *now choose life* by taking up our cross and following him.

SUGGESTED READING

☐ Read, one after the other: Deuteronomy
6:20–25, Mark 14:22–24, and 1 Corinthians
11:23–26.

Reflection

When you read the above passages, what do you notice? Does anything strike you from reading them together that you didn't notice before?

_____

_____

_____

_____

Much of the contemporary church focuses on making faith relevant, but at times this happens at the expense of remembering that ours is an ancient faith, too. How might the above passages teach us to see our faith as both ancient and relevant?

_____

_____

_____

_____

4

DEUTERONOMY 5–11: WORSHIP AS A MEANS OF KNOWING GOD

How does a person go from entering into relationship with God (Deut 1–4) to living faithfully before him (Deut 12–26)? Deuteronomy 5–11 seeks to provide an answer. It does so by identifying and then developing the hinge that turns decision into faithful living: *worship*.

The Face in the Pool

Worship is not something we understand well. Often we associate it with the things of Sunday services: singing, praying, and practicing rites. To be sure, these play an important role in worship, but they are not the whole of what worship is. The heart of worship, I would suggest, is far simpler: it is the *beholding* and *adoring* of something.

But beholding and adoring are not good in and of themselves; the thing they focus on determines whether they're good or bad. G. K. Beale has summarized this well: "What people revere, they resemble, either for ruin or

DEUTERONOMY 5–11: WORSHIP AS A MEANS OF KNOWING GOD 29

for restoration."[4] He does not mean this narrowly, as if lovers of money will turn into money themselves. He means instead that if we worship things other than God, then we, like figures of stone and wood, will become blind and deaf to God. This, in turn, will lead to the corruption of the worshiper as God's image-bearer.

Idolatry, then, is simply beholding and adoring the wrong thing. Yet the true danger of idolatry is far subtler than we think. We know the struggle for Western Christians is not about bowing down before figurines but about pursuing things like sex, money, power, and prestige. As we mature in our faith, we learn to guard against these. Where even mature Christians still stumble, though, is in believing idolatry lies strictly outside of worship. The most dangerous idolatry lies *within* worship.

Within worship we behold and adore God, so it is within worship that we learn what God is like (beholding) and commit ourselves to him (adoring). The problem, though, is that as humans our understanding of God tends to be skewed. Due to God's grand otherness, it is difficult for us to imagine him properly. What we tend to do instead, quite unwittingly, is imagine him in our own image and likeness. God begins to resemble our own needs and desires.

A powerful though haunting illustration of this dynamic is found in Greek mythology, the story of Narcissus. Narcissus was a young man of great beauty, and his beauty attracted much attention and many suitors. Yet the attention did not flatter Narcissus; it only caused him to grow proud. He became so proud that he spurned all suitors, disdaining and humiliating them. In more than one case the humiliation was so great that it destroyed the lives of the suitors.

This did not go unnoticed, and one day the goddess Nemesis decided to take revenge upon Narcissus. She conceived a trap that would bring upon Narcissus the very suffering he caused others. She lured him to a pool in the mountains so that he might look upon his own reflection—for Narcissus, never having seen his own appearance, would not recognize the face in the pool. So when the man lay down to drink, he was confronted by a face of incredible beauty. Finally, a suitor worthy of Narcissus' love! Narcissus was in love, enraptured by the face in the pool.

But try as he might, Narcissus could not get the person in the pool to respond. He lay for untold time staring at the image, obsessed and enflamed, speaking to it and pleading for it to speak back, begging for it to come out of the pool, plunging his arms in the water to grasp it, weeping over it. The man in the pool would never respond, but Narcissus continued to lie there staring into the pool. He could not free himself from the fixation, and as time went by he wasted away and died.

Many of us are like Narcissus. Believing we are worshiping God, we are actually gazing upon our own reflection. God looks strangely familiar to our own wants and needs. Though the object of our longing seems to be of immense importance, it only causes us to waste away. We are unable to free ourselves from the spell.

Worship as Prioritizing

Deuteronomy is well aware of this inclination, and it takes steps to guard against it. It does so, in chapters 5–11, by laying the foundations for true worship, showing what the worship of Yahweh ought to be like. These chapters begin with the Ten Commandments and then develop just two commands: the first and the second. Understanding how these fit together is vital to understanding the book's teaching on proper worship.

The Ten Commandments sit at the beginning of Deuteronomy 5–11 (5:7–21) and run as follows:

1. No other gods (v. 7)

2. No idols or images (v. 8–10)

3. No taking of the Lord's name in vain (v. 11)

4. Observing the Sabbath (v. 12–15)

5. Honoring mother and father (v. 16)

6. No murdering (v. 17)

7. No committing adultery (v. 18)

8. No stealing (v. 19)

9. No bearing false witness (v. 20)

10. No coveting (v. 21)

Commonly known as commands, these are more like ten *principles* of a constitution: a set of foundational principles to organize the life of the community. And just as a country's constitution reveals its values, so the Ten Commandments reveal the values of Israel.

Most revealing is the logic of the ten principles. They move from worship (1–4) to ethics (5–9) to desire (10). In other words, worship is the fountainhead of ethics and desire, and we must get it right if we hope to get the others right. To say it differently, we cannot hope to have good behavior or virtuous desires if we worship the wrong thing. In this sense, the Ten Commandments stand as a hierarchy of values or a hierarchy of desire.

As humans, we live our lives according to a hierarchy of desire that prioritizes the things we value and pursue. The most important things are at the top, the least important at the bottom, and everything else is in between. This is a good and necessary part of navigating life. Problems arise, though, when things from the bottom of the pyramid get placed at the top—that is, when insignificant things are given significance. The pyramid becomes top heavy and topples over. Imagine, for instance, a man who prioritizes his hobbies over his family: he gains a little free time at the cost of his wife and children.

The real danger, though, is in placing at the top those things that are good but not supreme. For example, think of financial stability, personal comfort, or family reputation. All of these are good and natural pursuits, but they are not ultimate pursuits. If a person pursues these above God, it will unsettle the hierarchy of desires and topple the pyramid. That is the reason for the Ten Commandments: they seek to build an appropriate hierarchy of desire in God's people, the top of which is love of God.

Have you ever wondered why the Ten Commandments were written on two stone tablets rather than one? There would have been a reason beyond the practical, for the words themselves did not require much space. One possibility is that the commands were divided evenly between the tablets, five on each. This would be supported by the idea that the number of the commands—ten—is meant to correspond to the number of a person's fingers for the purposes of memorization.[5] Two hands with five fingers, then, would correspond to two tablets with five commands each. Another possibility is that each tablet contained all ten commands. This would reflect the ancient practice associated with treaties, where each party would get a copy to keep. Since Deuteronomy reflects the conventions of ancient treaties in a number of ways already, this would not be surprising. Further, it would fit with the description of the tablets' storage in the ark of the covenant (Deut 10:1–5), which represented the relationship between God and Israel. The reason may be a combination of these as well, with all ten commands appearing on both tablets but the number ten being used so that the people might easily learn and remember them.

Worship as Adoring

Having established Israel's hierarchy of desire, Deuteronomy 5–11 goes on to develop the fountainhead of the hierarchy, worship, by focusing on the first two commandments. The first commandment prohibits the worship of other gods: "You shall have no other gods before me" (Deut 5:7). To say it positively, it calls for exclusive devotion to Yahweh.

This call is central to Deuteronomy's message and is a defining part of Israel's faith. Its foundational text, which Israelites recited to their children morning and night, is Deuteronomy 6:4-5:

> Hear, O Israel: The LORD our God, the LORD is one. Love the LORD your God with all your heart and with all your soul and with all your strength.

It is because of texts like this that Israel's faith is called "monotheism," meaning "one god." Monotheism, though, can be a misleading word, for it characterizes things in comparative terms: it is a call to worship the singular God Yahweh rather than the multiple gods of Israel's neighbors. To be sure, a key difference between Israel and their neighbors was their worship of one God. But this is not the primary issue in view here. The primary issue is not the nature of Yahweh but the *nature of Israel's worship* of him.

As such, the call to worship him as "one" concerns devotion. It is no accident that the closest linguistic parallel to Deuteronomy 6:4-5, in Hebrew, is found in the Song of Songs (italics added):

> My dove, my perfect one, is *the only one*,
> the only one of her mother,
> pure to her who bore her. (Song 6:9 ESV)

The idea here, as in Deuteronomy 6:4-5, focuses not so much on the number of the loved one but on the singular and exclusive love shown by the lover. In other words, the call to love Yahweh as one is the call to adore him as a groom does his bride. It is a radical and all-consuming adoration.

The enemies of such devotion are apathy and apostasy—that is, lukewarmness and infidelity. Both feature in the Bible, though infidelity, or idolatry, is the one that gets the most attention. It's also the one we struggle to identify with today. But that is because we don't understand idolatry.

In the biblical world, people did not bow down before wood and stone figurines; they bowed down before deities, represented in idols, in order to pledge allegiance to them. But why would someone leave Yahweh to pledge allegiance to some other god? We tend to forget the ancients had issues, just like us. They, too, had ailing parents, infertile spouses, and children with health problems. What's more, they frequently faced drought, famine, war, and injustice. The reason they ran to other gods, therefore, was because they felt Yahweh had failed to care for their basic needs. They hoped that another god might provide for their family's basic health and welfare. If any of us has been tempted, for the sake of loved ones, to put our trust in someone or something questionable, then we will understand Israel's dilemma. For instance, when a father tends toward workaholism, he typically does so because he thinks it will secure a better future for his family.

Worship as Beholding

Even if a person remains wholly devoted to God, another issue still remains: how does she know the God she worships is the true God and not one of her own making? Few of us, for example, could fault the *devotion* of the members of Westboro Baptist Church, who protest the funerals of

fallen soldiers with incendiary signs. Yet few of us would
find their idea of God to be good or true, either. This example shows why the principle of the first commandment
must always work with the principle of the second: it
is not enough to be devoted to something; we must be
devoted to the right thing. And we become devoted to the
right thing by beholding God rightly in worship.

The second commandment sets out this principle by
banning the use of images in worship, which is called
"aniconism," meaning "no icons" (Deut 5:8-9):

> You shall not make for yourself an image in
> the form of anything in heaven above or on
> the earth beneath or in the waters below.
> You shall not bow down to them or wor-
> ship them.

To this day, there are a variety of opinions on how we
should apply this command, ranging from banning images
wholesale to encouraging icons in worship and only banning images of God the Father. What often gets lost in the
shuffle is the *intent* of the command.

Whatever its application, the command's intent is to
guard against the misrepresentation of Yahweh. Since
Israel's neighbors used images and figurines in the worship of their gods, the concern was that Israel would do
the same. But in doing so, Israel would ultimately distort
the person of Yahweh. For how can an earthen image cap-
ture the God of the universe without diminishing him?
How can a deaf, dumb, and stationary statue represent the
God who listens, speaks, and acts? The command's concern, therefore, is deeply practical: if our representations

distort God, then the object of our worship is something other than God.

The issue for Israel and us is not in believing that a stone statue is God but in imagining God wrongly. As A. W. Tozer has said,

> The history of mankind will probably show that no people has ever risen above its religion, and man's spiritual history will positively demonstrate that no religion has ever been greater than its idea of God. For this reason the gravest question before the Church is always God Himself, and the most portentous fact about any man is not what he at a given time may say or do, but what he in his deep heart conceives God to be like. We tend by a secret law of the soul to move toward our mental image of God.[6]

Since worship is where we behold God, it is also where we learn to imagine him rightly. And since how we imagine God determines our imitation of him, representing him rightly is of the utmost importance. That is why Deuteronomy replaces images and icons with memory. By remembering God's goodness to Israel in the past and his promises for them in the future, the people represented God truly.

Knowing God through Worship

So worship is central in moving God's people from the point of decision to the practice of right living. But how do we, as Christians, parlay these concepts from

Deuteronomy into our lives today? That is, how do we learn to adore God completely and behold him rightly? Perhaps the greatest tool is the practice of taking inventory. By this I mean intentionally observing our own interior lives and external habits, both as individuals and communities, to see what we prize and how we portray God.

But how do we take inventory of our devotion? It's actually easier than we might think. We only need to learn to identify those things that occupy our thoughts and longings, and we can do so by asking ourselves two questions: *What animates me most? What agitates me most?* These will get to the heart of things very quickly.

What you'll probably learn is that the things occupying your heart and mind are not the notorious taboos. Do people struggle with things such as drugs, alcohol, and gambling? Yes, but the culprits for most of us are more commonplace: finances, children, personal appearance, social standing. Cosmetics and beauty products, get-rich-quick schemes, children's schools—the immensity of the industries and marketing surrounding such things witness to their place in our lives. What makes them dangerous is that they are, at some level, *good*. Who doesn't want good education and opportunities for their children? Who doesn't want their family to have financial stability?

We want such things because they're good. But they become bad, even idolatrous, when given positions of ultimate significance in our lives. How can we tell? A good indicator is when they cause undue distress. Do you find yourself easily angered about finances, sometimes lashing out at loved ones? Do you experience gripping anxiety

over everyday decisions for your children, perhaps caus-
ing problems with sleeping or eating? While these scenar-
ios have become increasingly common in Western society,
they are not healthy—and they demand that we take steps
to reorient their place of influence. That will require
practical steps, such as accountability with friends and
counseling. But it will also require good, old-fashioned
confession before God: confide in him your worry, and
ask him to help you balance the responsibilities he has
entrusted to you with your worship of him as the great
Provider.

Once we arrange the hierarchy of our devotions, we
must take stock of how we imagine God. For even if we
find God at the center of our soul, we must ask, "God who?"
The simple reality is that, as humans, we tend to make God
in our own image. So even if we are truly devoted to God
as we imagine him, he may not be the God of Scripture
but one of our own making—a yes man, tyrant, or worse.

How we imagine God, therefore, is an issue of acute
importance, both personally and communally. Personally,
our imaginings of God can be paralyzing if we see him
too negatively—as an overbearing parent or a harsh
judge—and they can be enabling if we see him too lib-
erally—as a yes man or an indulgent uncle saying, "God
just wants me to be happy!" Communally, our images
of God are writ large in church and society, often in the
form of strife and dysfunction. Notable examples dot
the landscape of church history: for instance, influen-
tial medieval monk Bernard of Clairvaux supporting the
Crusades of the Middle Ages and the state church supporting Nazism in Germany. Though complete devotion

and right representation are both ingredients of worship, representation is most essential. The most damage is done not through apathy but zealotry—zealotry based on a skewed idea of God.

So while the symptoms may be many and complicated, the underlying disease is simple. Tozer describes it thus:

> Before the church goes into eclipse any-
> where there must first be a corrupting of
> her simple basic theology. She simply gets
> a wrong answer to the question, "What is
> God like?" and goes on from there. Though
> she may continue to cling to a sound nom-
> inal creed, her practical working creed has
> become false. The masses of her adherents
> come to believe that God is different from
> what He actually is.[7]

We might reasonably ask how to fight against this disease. Again we must take inventory, monitoring how exactly we do imagine God. Once we've identified a skewed image, we must remove it and replace it with a biblical one. As C. S. Lewis himself said, "My idea of God is not a divine idea. It has to be shattered time after time."[8]

A good place to begin is with Jesus of Nazareth, the "image of the invisible God" (Col 1:15). First, read through the four Gospels in one sitting, following Jesus through the key moments of his life and letting them forge in your mind an enduring image. After this, return to the Gospels, now reading individual episodes very slowly and delib-erately. A helpful approach here is an approach called Ignatian contemplation. This is part of the legacy of Saint

Ignatius, a renowned spiritual guide during the Middle Ages, and is essentially *imaginative prayer*. It invites readers to contemplate a single episode from Christ's life in such a way as to see yourself there as a participant rather than observer: What would it have been like? The sights, sounds, smells? How would I have felt witnessing this? [9] The experience, in turn, is meant to draw people closer to Christ, to create a closer walk with him and a desire to speak with him in prayer.

SUGGESTED READING

☐ Deuteronomy 5:8–9

☐ Colossians 1:15–20

☐ John 1:14; 1 John 1:1–3

Reflection

Before reading this chapter, what was your understanding of the Old Testament's ban on representing God with images?

_____

_____

_____

_____

How now would you explain, in your own words, the importance of this ban?

_____

_____

_____

_____

In light of the above New Testament passages, what is the role of Christ in helping us to know the invisible God?

_____

_____

_____

_____

5

DEUTERONOMY 12– 26: LAW AS A MEANS OF KNOWING GOD

If Deuteronomy 5–11 shows us how, in worship, we can know God truly, then Deuteronomy 12–26 shows us how to live in light of that knowledge. Many will wonder how Deuteronomy 12–26, the legal section of Deuteronomy, speaks to Christian living. After all, didn't Christ free us from the burden of the law? Yes and no. Christ freed us from one part of the law: the need to maintain the covenant through ceremony and sacrifice. But the part he did not free us from, and in fact came to model, was holiness. So while many still see the law as a cage to constrain, we may also see it as scaffolding to sanctification—the framework by which we can learn to live holy lives.

Knowing through Doing

But how exactly does the law teach us to be godly? For most of us, "education" refers to learning through the mind: for example, learning to read or to do arithmetic. But there are other ways of learning as well. One is the

kind we acquire through *doing*—that is, through perform-
ing activities over and over until our bodies, rather than
our minds, have mastered its knowledge. This kind of
learning, I suggest, is how the law teaches holiness.

Typically, we associate bodily learning with practical
or technical skills. In the Western world, many of us grew
up in a time when the mastery of two such skills, cursive
writing and bicycle riding, marked important points in
childhood development. Yet for such simple skills, the
learning of these was often accompanied by much friction and frustration.

I suspect, though, that the friction reveals something
about the learning that needed to take place. An adult can
explain until they're blue in the face, but a child can only
learn cursive writing or bike riding through *doing*. Sure,
parents and teachers can give tips, but even these will be
bodily in nature: "this is what it should *look* like" or "this is
how it will *feel*." The friction comes from them trying, and
failing, to teach with words what must be learned with the
body. We only learned by practicing the activity—over and
over and over. And once we did so, our knowledge was no
less real than our knowledge of arithmetic, though it will
be far less explainable. The widespread presence of such
knowledge is why we have the proverb of things being
"like riding a bike."

Or consider another form of bodily learning: childhood chores. Growing up, my sisters and I had household
chores to do nightly and weekly. They included things
like vacuuming, washing dishes, feeding the dogs, and
mowing the lawn. If our tasks weren't completed, there
were consequences: no TV, no pocket money, no playing

next door. Despite our suspicions, the point of the chores was not to keep house through cheap child labor. The point was to engrain in us children certain virtues, values, and attitudes.

Through chores, the home became a training ground for life outside of its doors. The hope was not merely that, as adults, we would continue to clean our dishes or mow our lawns. The hope was that the virtues, values, and attitudes we learned through these would translate into other realms as well—that we would grow from good family members into good citizens of country and world. But such things cannot be learned in theory; they must be learned in practice. People don't learn to value community service through listening to lectures but through washing their sister's dishes; they don't learn to value work by watching others work but by pushing a lawn mower under the heat of the summer sun.

This, then, is how the law teaches holiness: it requires people to practice habits and observe rituals, over and over, in order to engrain in them certain values and attitudes. In this way, religious rituals are more than a means to an end, such as achieving atonement or purification. While they can become so, they are also more than "empty rituals" or "hollow observations." Instead, they are like childhood chores in that they deposit in our bodies a kind of knowledge we can gain in no other way.

The Law: A Tutor in Gratefulness

What values and dispositions does Deuteronomy deposit in our bodies? Most of us imagine the legal material as detailing the dreariest of affairs, but this is not the case.

A fair part of it focuses on feasts and festivals. Yet its concern is not that these will be too lifeless, but too lively—that the feasts and festivals will be celebrated for the wrong reason, as revelry rather than worship. For this reason, a unique goal in Deuteronomy is to engrain *joy* and *gratefulness* in the people as they celebrate.

More than any other section of Scripture, Deuteronomy 12–26 focuses on the land. To be more precise, it looks at the land as Yahweh's inheritance gift to Israel (*nahalah*). This gift of the land, though, comes with conditions. It is a gift given with a purpose—namely, to become the place on the planet where God is embodied most fully. In order

Deuteronomy 12 looks forward to a time when the people would worship the Lord in the land, which it speaks of as the "place the LORD will choose" and "dwelling for his Name" (12:5, 11, 14, 18, 21, 26). Deuteronomy itself does not name this place, but we now know it would be Jerusalem and that the dwelling for his name would be the temple there. The idea that Yahweh's name would dwell in the temple meant that he would be its owner and reside there and that people could come there to meet with him in worship. But the meaning is not merely abstract, as we have learned from archaeological discoveries. It appears now that this reflects a broader practice from the ancient world, where rulers would literally write their name on the foundation stone of buildings they had commissioned.[10] The purpose was not just to stamp it as their property, but to signal that it was to be used according to their values and desires. Anything else would be to disrespect the one whose name dwelled there.

to accomplish this, Israel must worship Yahweh rightly
and embody him through righteousness and social justice.

One of the keys to doing this is keeping the land in
proper perspective. While idols and foreign religion
pose real risks, the one risk we miss is the *land itself*.
Deuteronomy 8 describes it well:

> When you have eaten and are satisfied,
> praise the LORD your God for the good land
> he has given you. Be careful that you do not
> forget the LORD your God, failing to observe
> his commands, his laws and his decrees that
> I am giving you this day. Otherwise, when
> you eat and are satisfied, when you build
> fine houses and settle down, and when your
> herds and flocks grow large and your silver
> and gold increase and all you have is mul-
> tiplied, then your heart will become proud
> and you will forget the LORD your God,
> who brought you out of Egypt, out of the
> land of slavery. He led you through the vast
> and dreadful wilderness, that thirsty and
> waterless land, with its venomous snakes
> and scorpions. He brought you water out
> of hard rock. He gave you manna to eat in
> the wilderness, something your ancestors
> had never known, to humble and test you
> so that in the end it might go well with you.
> You may say to yourself, "My power and the
> strength of my hands have produced this
> wealth for me." But remember the LORD your
> God, for it is he who gives you the ability to

> produce wealth, and so confirms his cove-
> nant, which he swore to your ancestors, as
> it is today. (8:10–18)

Deuteronomy envisions a time in the not-too-distant future when the people will be tempted to see the land as a monument to their own achievement.

How can Israel avoid falling into this trap? The answer given by Deuteronomy 8 is twofold: by practicing *memory* and *thanksgiving.* As Israel lives in the freedom and blessing of the land, they must remember their past in Egypt and the wilderness—which is to say, their past slavery and deprivation. It is by remembering that Israel will preserve a proper perspective, for it will keep them from exalting themselves (v. 14). A "humbled" Israel will recognize that it was *God* "who brought you out of Egypt, out of the land of slavery" and God who provided the sustenance of life in the wilderness (vv. 3, 14). With this perspective in place, Israel will be able to fulfill the second aspect: thanksgiving. The memories of Egypt and the wilderness will allow them to "praise the LORD your God for the good land he has given you" (v. 10). In short, Israel should view the land as a gift, not an entitlement, and God as the giver.

Deuteronomy 12 and 16 provide windows into the manner in which Israel was to practice memory and thanksgiving. Chapter 12 focuses on the chosen place where all Israel would gather for worship. Yet the emphasis here is not on the place itself, which is why no specific location is named. The emphasis is on the purpose of the place: to be the dwelling place for the Lord's "Name" (12:5). Despite its mystical sound, the intention is quite practical here:

> The essential point ... is faithfulness to
> Yahweh. The true place of worship is one
> that is known to belong wholly and unequiv-
> ocally to Yahweh.[11]

In other words, by having his name dwell in this place,
Yahweh promises to "belong wholly and unequivocally"
to the people, and they in turn are to belong wholly and
unequivocally to him. The chosen place, therefore, is
where Yahweh meets his people, shaping them into his
image-bearers.

The chapter goes on to develop how such shaping
occurs, emphasizing the nature of the people's worship
in the chosen place:

> But you are to seek the place the LORD your
> God will choose from among all your tribes to
> put his Name there for his dwelling. To that
> place you must go; there bring your burnt
> offerings and sacrifices, your tithes and spe-
> cial gifts, what you have vowed to give and
> your freewill offerings, and the firstborn of
> your herds and flocks. There, in the presence
> of the LORD your God, you and your families
> shall eat and shall rejoice in everything you
> have put your hand to, because the LORD
> your God has blessed you. (12:5–7)

The central activity, we notice, is the bringing of produce
of the land as offerings before God. This is not incidental,
for it reveals the heart of the rituals: for Israel to recognize
God's gift of the land by sacrificing a small portion of it
to him in worship.

Yet for Deuteronomy it is not enough for the people merely to perform these activities; they must also have the right disposition. That is why we find the most unusual of commands here: *rejoice*! Three times Deuteronomy 12 commands the Israelites to rejoice in worship (vv. 7, 12, 18). Each of these follows a set of instructions on worshiping, when people would bring their offerings to sacrifice before God followed by a shared feast with some of the produce and meat. The point, it seems, is that the worship is not complete in the act of sacrificing. An Israelite would be tempted to see the situation as comprised of two parts: a sacrifice for God and a feast for the people. But Deuteronomy is clear that the act of worship is only truly complete when the worshiper has *enjoyed* it.

But how can Deuteronomy *command* something such as joy? Is it possible to demand that someone should feel a certain way? Strange as it sounds, yes, it is possible. More to the point in Deuteronomy, we can actually train ourselves to feel certain ways in certain situations. That's where Deuteronomy 16 comes into play.

Deuteronomy 16 outlines Israel's three pilgrimage feasts: the Feast of Passover (or Unleavened Bread), the Feast of Weeks, and the Feast of Booths. These were the three times each year when the Israelites would travel from their farms and villages to worship at the chosen place. What is not apparent to most of us is the central, theological purpose at the heart of the festive calendar: it was meant to commemorate Israel's exodus journey.

In celebrating the three festivals, then, Israel would annually reenact the journey from Egypt, through the wilderness, into the promised land. Key to the commemorations is the way in which they characterize the events in certain moods. Passover, on the one hand, commemorated Egypt and the wilderness, and it cast these in the mood of hardship and sorrow. For example (all italics added):

> Eat unleavened bread, *the bread of affliction*, because you left Egypt in haste—so that all the days of your life you may remember the time of your departure from Egypt. (16:3)

> Offer the Passover sacrifice, *in the evening at sunset*, at the time you came out of Egypt. (16:6 ESV)

> Then in the morning return to *your tents*. (16:7)

These might seem incidental, but they are part of Deuteronomy's effort to portray the feast in a somber mood. It quite literally occurs in darkness, and its food recalls a time of "affliction" and its setting a time of land- less "tent" dwelling.

In stark contrast, the Feasts of Weeks and Booths both focused on the joy of living in the land. It is not an acci- dent that they occured at key points in the agricultural calendar: the beginning and end of harvest, respectively. The Feast of Weeks celebrated the beginning of the har- vest season, when the first of the grain produce had come ready, and Booths the end of the harvest, when figs, dates, olives, and grapes were gathered. Whereas Passover used food to recall affliction, here food is the source of joy. Indeed, joy is the thing that ought to characterize each feast (16:11, 14). Yet joy is more than mere emotion;

here, as elsewhere in Deuteronomy, joy equals gratefulness. Gratefulness to God, in turn, is shown in generosity
toward others. That is why Deuteronomy sees in the feasts
a time of rejoicing before God and generosity toward the
less fortunate. Just as God was generous to Israel, so Israel
shall be generous to others.

In Deuteronomy the law acts as a tutor teaching gratefulness. It trains people through the repetition of ritual
not only how to act but also how to *feel*. In this sense, the
law is like children's chores: through basic acts of obedience, a person begins to embody certain values and
attitudes in hope that these will grow into greater expres-
sions of godliness.

Knowing God through Obedience

A timelier message would be hard to find, for this speaks
to the heart of our world today. Most of us have far more
than we'll ever need, yet we're tempted to feel jealous
when our neighbor gets a new car or our friends a new
kitchen. We feel slighted when a coworker gets the pro-
motion or recognized for an award. We're good at hiding,
even sanctifying, these feelings, but at the end of the day,
it's simple: we're *ungrateful*. The human creature is one
that constantly compares, desiring what others have while
forgetting one's own blessings. If Deuteronomy is to be
believed, the tendency toward ingratitude is an insidious
one.

What can we to do? We can do worse, I suspect, than
follow the example of Deuteronomy: practicing *remembrance* and *thanksgiving*. That is to say, to intentionally
reflect on what has been and what we now have, in order

to recognize God's hand in it all. In so doing, we create in ourselves a perspective of gratitude.

Such practices can take many forms and frequencies. It is important, though, that they have *some* frequency, for it is through repetition that gratitude is engrained in our bodies. An example of a weekly practice is one my family does every Sunday: as we take our walk along a local path, we speak with each other and the children about things we're grateful for—my job, our home, food on the table, etc. Inevitably this leads to us recalling when I didn't have a job or had a bad one, or when we didn't have a house and had to live in various one-room rentals as a family. It's likely the kids won't remember those times, so it's important that we help them remember in order that they don't assume such things can be expected as entitlements.

My wife and I also cast the net more broadly, historically and globally, discussing things such as how our great-grandparents came by wagon to settle and farm the land or how other children in the world live today. As part of the process, we ask our children what they're thankful for. In all of this, of course, we seek to recognize God's hand in things. We also try to link this gratitude in the children with our charitable service to others, so that they know precisely how the gratitude to God and service to others are connected.

Perhaps the most obvious though often overlooked way to practice gratitude is the Lord's Supper. It's the ultimate embodiment of gratitude, as its name itself reveals: "Eucharist" comes from the Greek for "thanksgiving." So in partaking of the body and blood, we are at once remembering Christ's crucifixion and giving thanks for its blessing to us. It is in this way, then, that we can fulfill what the Westminster Confession, tweaked by John Piper, calls the chief end of man: to glorify God *by* enjoying him forever.[12]

SUGGESTED READING

☐ Deuteronomy 8:10–18

☐ John 15:9–17

☐ Romans 1:18–32

Reflection

What has been your own understanding of Old Testament law? Where does this understanding come from?

_____

_____

_____

_____

Had you ever considered before that religious practices might have a positive role, namely to cultivate godly virtues and attitudes? How have you seen this put into practice in your own life or the lives of others around you?

_____

_____

_____

_____

When you read the above Bible passages, what is the connection between gratitude/thanksgiving to God and joy/love toward others? What is the significance of that connection?

_____

_____

_____

_____

6

DEUTERONOMY 27–34: COVENANT AS A MEANS OF KNOWING GOD

Deuteronomy 27–34 concludes the book by focusing on a challenge facing Israel: living life in the land but without Moses. Moses will soon die, and his absence will leave a leadership vacuum in Israel. He makes provision for this in a number of ways, but his most important role, as covenant mediator, is the trickiest to address. Perhaps that is why these final chapters, even while making practical provisions, shift the focus back to the heart of the matter: the covenant itself. It is as if Moses is telling the people that, in the end, they themselves must learn to trust Yahweh. Originally, Moses stood in the gap when the people were afraid (Deut 5:5, 23–27), but now they must do it for themselves. In this way, Deuteronomy portrays the covenant itself as the environment in which Israel can come to know God better.

Knowing through Commitment

Relationships, like trees, need time and space to grow. They need a stable and safe environment in which they can grow, get pruned, and grow again without the worry of being chopped down at the first sight of imperfections. Relationships, like some trees, take years and years to begin producing fruit. The question, then, is how to create an environment in which such a thing can grow. The answer is *a solemn promise*.

Lewis Smedes has written simply and beautifully on how promises accomplish this feat:

> When a woman makes a promise, she thrusts her hand into the unpredictable circumstances of her tomorrow and creates an enclave of predictable reality. When a man makes a promise, he creates an island of certainty in a heaving ocean of uncertainty ... when you make a promise you have created a small sanctuary of trust within the jungle of unpredictability.[13]

At the heart of his word-pictures lies one basic idea: in making a promise, we create for someone else a safe place in an unsafe world.

The most amazing part of a promise is how it actually creates this safe place. "We take it on our feeble wills to keep a future rendezvous with someone in circumstances we cannot possibly predict."[14] In other words, the act is deeply personal in that you offer nothing other than yourself. You do not offer ways or means for overcoming adversity; you do not offer strategies for finding prosperity. You offer only yourself, and this offer, remarkably, gives the person "an island of certainty."

In this "sanctuary of trust," then, we enter a unique environment of learning about each other. On the one hand, we come to discover our own true identity: "Maybe we can best find out who and what we are by asking about the promises we have made to other people and the promises we are trying to keep for their sakes."[15] On the other hand, we come to discover who our partner is as they travel the same journey. What we find here is a great paradox: that by binding ourselves through promises we can enter relationships where we're free to be ourselves.

I think here of a conversation I had with my grandparents after their sixty-fifth wedding anniversary. They were asking how long my wife and I had been married. We said it had been twelve years. "Oh! I barely knew your grandpa after that long!" my grandma said. "In fact, I'm not sure I began to know him until after thirty years, and even then it wasn't until fifty years that I truly understood the man."

"Lord, I'm glad I didn't know what I was getting into back then," my grandpa said. "If I had known half of what I was in for ..."

"Oh, you!" my grandma cut in.

The conversation was quite entertaining and continued on, but at some point something struck me: their original commitment to each other, in marriage vows, was what provided the *environment* for them to come to know each other. Without such an environment, it stands to reason, such knowing might never have happened. This runs against the common practice today where young people are increasingly cohabiting in order to decide whether they want to promise themselves in marriage. But if it is the promises that provide the safe environment, then such learning cannot happen outside of such promises.

We might say the same of the covenant between God and his people: its promises provide the environment in which we can know and be known. In Smedes's words, then, we can hear the address of God to his covenant people:

> My people, the ones who belong to me, who depend on me, also know me by the promises I have made. What I promise is what I am and will be to them. Only if they really know what I am can they live with me in trust. They know me ... by knowing my power to keep promises.[16]

If this is true, then we can only come to know God through making and keeping our promises to him.

Covenant: An Environment for Learning

Through this view, the material of Deuteronomy 27–34 takes on new light. True, these chapters outline mechanisms by which the covenant is to be kept central in Moses' absence. But beneath these formal structures runs a deeper current. The reason the mechanisms are important is because they preserve the promises, and the promises are the environment in which Israel will come to know Yahweh *truly*. As such, these mechanisms are the means by which Israel will remember the covenant promises—their promise to Yahweh and Yahweh's promise to them.

The most prominent mechanism is the covenant-renewal ceremony, which is detailed in Deuteronomy 27–28. Moses tells the people how they are to renew their covenant commitment once they enter the land. It is no accident that the ceremony will take place at Shechem. It was there that Abram, having journeyed from his homeland, encountered God again: "To your offspring I will give this land" (Gen 12:7). In response, Abraham built an altar to commemorate the fact that God had appeared to him there to confirm his previous promises. As such, Shechem has deep significance, for it represents the place *par excellence* that covenantal promises are made and confirmed. When Moses instructs the Israelites to gather there, he is tying the covenant at Mount Sinai into the already-ancient covenant with Abraham.

> The site of ancient Shechem lies just outside of the modern city of Nablus in the West Bank, with Mount Ebal sitting to the north and Mount Gerizim to the south. Intriguingly, recent decades have seen the excavation of ancient ruins on Mount Ebal that bear resemblance to the ceremony detailed in Deuteronomy 27 and recorded in Joshua 8:30–35. Debate continues over the exact identification of these ruins, but there are several key features that match the biblical descriptions: it is located on Mount Ebal, dates to around 1200 BC, is a structure of uncut stone that was used for burning items, and contains the bones of animals reflective of the Israelite diet and religious sacrifices at that time.[17] Furthermore, this is the only site for some distance that bears all of these features.

The ceremony itself was rather involved. To begin with, the twelve tribes would divide in half and take their place at the bases of the two mountains flanking Shechem, Mounts Ebal and Gerizim. From Mount Gerizim, six tribes would pronounce across the valley the covenant blessings; from Mount Ebal, the other six tribes would pronounce back the curses. Then the tribes would gather on Mount Ebal, building an altar on which to sacrifice and erecting stones upon which to inscribe the law. In this way, Israel would inscribe upon its own heart the promise it had made to Yahweh.

Another mechanism Moses commands is the preservation and public reading of the book of the law:

> So Moses wrote down this law and gave it to the Levitical priests, who carried the ark of the covenant of the LORD, and to all the elders of Israel. Then Moses commanded them: "At the end of every seven years, in the year for canceling debts, during the Festival of Tabernacles, when all Israel comes to appear before the LORD your God at the place he will choose, you shall read this law before them in their hearing. Assemble the people—men, women and children, and the foreigners residing in your towns—so they can listen and learn to fear the LORD your God and follow carefully all the words of this law. Their children, who do not know this law, must hear it and learn to fear the LORD your God as long as you live in the

land you are crossing the Jordan to possess."
(Deut 31:9-13)

This reflects a common convention in ancient treaties called a document clause. It was to ensure the people would continue to know and observe the stipulations of the formal relationship.

Yet it would be a mistake to overlook a key difference between Deuteronomy and other ancient treaties: it uses the convention religiously rather than politically. It takes the practice of public reading and brings it into the service of the covenant, meaning it occurs as an act of worship. During the Feast of Tabernacles, every seven years, Israel would stand at the chosen place and listen to words of the law. The express purpose was to "listen and learn to fear the LORD" and "follow carefully all the words of this law" (Deut 31:12). But there is something more in this practice: each time the people would hear the story of their journey with God—his deliverance, his goodness, his mercy, his self-revelation, his compassion. In short, the people would hear the history of promises—promises made and promises kept.

The final mechanism we find is a song. "Now write down this song and teach it to the Israelites and have them sing it, so that it may be a witness for me against them. ... It will not be forgotten by their descendants" (Deut 31:19, 21). This is the most interesting of the mechanisms, for it was apparently taught by God to Moses and then by Moses to the people.

The song itself (Deut 32), often called the Song of Moses, is sweeping in style. It moves rapidly from Israel's

early history with God through to the future, when Israel
will rebel and be punished. It is not a flattering song, at
least not for Israel. The song develops by contrasting the
two covenant partners: Yahweh and Israel. Yahweh is portrayed as a good and faithful father, Israel as a spoiled and
rebellious child:

> Is he not your Father, your Creator,
>> who made you and formed you? (32:6)

> In a desert land he found him,
>> in a barren and howling waste.
> He shielded him and cared for him;
>> he guarded him as the apple of his eye.
> (v. 10)

> Jeshurun grew fat and kicked;
>> filled with food, they became heavy
>>> and sleek.
> They abandoned the God who made them
>> and rejected the Rock their Savior. (v. 15)

The Lord speaks of his anger toward his children and the
punishments that he plans. He even vows to hide his face
(v. 20).

But then a change takes place, and Yahweh relents of
his plans. He seems to remember his ancient promises
and, in a sudden turn, vows something supremely beau-
tiful (Deut 32:36-39):

> The LORD will vindicate his people
>> and relent concerning his servants
> when he sees their strength is gone
>> and no one is left, slave or free.

He will say: "Now where are their gods,
    the rock they took refuge in,
the gods who ate the fat of their sacrifices
    and drank the wine of their
        drink offerings?
Let them rise up to help you!
    Let them give you shelter!
"See now that I myself am he!
    There is no god besides me.
I put to death and I bring to life,
    I have wounded and I will heal,
and no one can deliver out of my hand."

The imagery is that of a wife who has gone after other lovers only to find herself abandoned and alone in the end. Then, from nowhere, her husband returns to take her home.

More than anywhere else in Deuteronomy, here we witness the depths of knowing that can come through a committed relationship. The relationship is based on a promise and that promise has been broken; the relationship has been ruptured, the sanctuary of trust shattered. Yet even in this a choice remains for the aggrieved party: they can leave, or they can stay. Because the offense happened to them, to them belongs the choice whether to heal the rupture, for they alone bear the wounds. If they choose to restore the rupture, they will do so in a confronting way: by renewing *their* original promises. Though they did not violate the promises, it is their promises that must be renewed. And that is what the Lord does here. He returns to Israel and renews his promises to her, restoring the sanctuary of trust. In this Israel learns something of God that they never could have learned otherwise: he is not only faithful but also *longsuffering*. This reality is seen most powerfully when it takes on flesh and bones in the book of Hosea.

Knowing God through Covenant

Covenant, then, provides a unique environment in which God's people can come to know him better, for it is stable and safe. This idea itself is a challenge to most of us. We tend to see covenant, at best, as a container in which relationship happens or, at worst, as a chamber in which captives are kept. But as we have discussed, the promises on which the covenant is built are the life-giving force behind it. The moment we pledge ourselves to God, a sphere of protection surrounds us; from there onward, though the world around us rages, we are safe within the sphere to learn about ourselves and our Lord. To me, a chief lesson here is that we retrain our minds to imagine covenant more fruitfully.

Since the Lord's Supper is the place at which Christians renew the covenant, it is also the place to begin retraining our minds. First of all, we must imagine the event as a recommitment to the "sanctuary of trust." Too often we come to it as mere penitence. And while penitence plays a role, it does so within the larger goals of the covenant: to know and be known. As such, we confess our failings in order to move forward together. This is true in any relationship.

Secondly, we must reflect on the deep history of the covenant. The great advantage of the biblical covenant over, say, common marriage covenants is that it possesses an ancient account of our partner's behavior. In other words, we have more than his promises; we have his entire history of relationships. And what does it show? Over the course of thousands of years, God has shown himself gracious, faithful, and loving.

More than that, he has shown himself patient and longsuffering. What was sung in the Song of Moses and embodied in Hosea and Gomer took on flesh in the person of Christ. He demonstrated his radical commitment to us, his covenant partners, in the crucifixion. When we come to the Eucharist, we will do well to remember: here we commit ourselves again to the covenant with Christ. In so doing, we remain in a safe sanctuary wherein we are invited to know and be known.

SUGGESTED READING

☐ Deuteronomy 32:10–18

☐ Hosea 11:1–8

☐ Matthew 23:37–39

Reflection

Before reading this chapter, what was your understanding of covenant?

_____

_____

_____

How does the idea of covenant as a "sanctuary of trust" change how we look at covenant in the Bible?

_____

_____

_____

In light of the above passages, what do we learn about the characteristics of God and his people as covenant partners?

_____

_____

_____

7

JESUS AND DEUTERONOMY: GRACE AS A MEANS OF KNOWING GOD

The one thing we have yet to consider is how Deuteronomy looks forward to the person of Christ. This is really a question of how the old covenant, mediated by Moses, relates to the new covenant, ushered in by Christ's crucifixion. The difficulty lies in the messages of the two covenants, which sometimes seem like opposites—like one covenant is characterized by legal stipulations and sanctions and another by grace and mercy. Yet as we shall see, they are not so different after all, for both Deuteronomy and the New Testament ground the hope of humanity in the very same thing: God's grace.

A Deeper Magic

In *The Lion, the Witch, and the Wardrobe*, C. S. Lewis develops the idea of "Deep Magic" and "deeper" magic,[18] an idea helpful for understanding how Deuteronomy looks forward to Christ. Things begin when one of the boys, Edmund, betrays his friends and family to the White Witch. He does so simply because he feels his siblings don't appreciate him enough—unlike the Witch, who pays him all kinds of attention. He doesn't realize until it's too late that the Witch has ulterior motives. Sure enough, as soon as Edmund is no longer useful to her, the Witch goes to Aslan demanding a bounty. Apparently, the Witch served as the "Emperor's hangman," as Mr. Beaver put it, and could collect the life of any person who committed treachery. Since Edmund betrayed his friends, she was entitled to his life.

When Aslan acknowledges the Witch's claim, the others erupt in protest. Susan, Edmund's sister, asks, "Can't we do something about the Deep Magic? Isn't there something we can work against it?" Aslan says little in response, other than stating that nothing can be done. But the Witch says more: "He knows the Deep Magic better than that. He knows that unless I have the blood as the Law says all Narnia will be overturned and perish in fire and water." This Deep Magic, or Law, is written into the very fabric of Narnian life, engraved on the Table of Stone, the fire-stones on the Secret Hill, and the scepter of the Emperor-beyond-the-Sea. This law is not hers, but the Emperor's.

Aslan then tells everyone to fall back while he speaks to the Witch alone. Upon his return, though, he reports, "She has renounced her claim on your brother's blood." The sharp contrast between this report and the demands of Deep Magic means a question now looms large: how can both Deep Magic be satisfied and Edmund be spared? It sets the stage for what will come.

The answer comes when Aslan forfeits himself to the Witch in Edmund's place. She has Aslan bound and placed upon the Stone Table, where she kills him with a stone blade. After everyone leaves, though, the stone table cracks in two, and the "great cracking, deafening noise" brings Susan and Lucy back to the place. What they find is the table broken and empty—no Aslan. And Susan utters the famous words: "What does it mean? Is it more magic?"

From behind the two girls comes a voice, saying, "Yes! It is more magic." And there stands the resurrected Aslan. With the girls struggling to comprehend the meaning of the events, Aslan explains:

> It means ... that though the Witch knew the Deep Magic, there is a magic deeper still which she did not know. Her knowledge goes back only to the dawn of time. But if she could have looked a little further back, into the stillness and darkness before Time dawned, she would have read there a different incantation. She would have known that when a willing victim who had committed no treachery was killed in a traitor's stead, the Table would crack and Death itself would start working backward.

From here onward, death does indeed work backward, with the Witch's work being undone and the land returning to its former flourishing.

One of the richest mines for interpreting Scripture is art and literature from church history. This is called "reception history"—the study of how different people in different ages have received, treasured, and interpreted the Bible. C. S. Lewis is a figure known to many evangelicals, but there are countless others that have wrestled with the mysteries of Scripture and helped unlock its secrets. The frescos in the catacombs of Rome; the Byzantine mosaics throughout the Middle East; the art and architecture of medieval cathedrals across Europe; the literature of medieval writers, such as Dante's *Inferno* and Milton's *Paradise Lost*; the writings of contemporary authors such as Flannery O'Connor or Wendell Berry—these are just the tip of the iceberg. A helpful place to begin, for English literature at least, is *A Dictionary of Biblical Tradition in English Literature*.[19]

Deuteronomy and a Deeper Magic

Lewis's chief insight is in his portrait of law and grace and the relationship between them. As he characterizes it, the law (Deep Magic) is not bad but good, for it comes from the very hand of God (the Emperor) and reveals something of his character. It can no more be discarded than the laws of gravity, for, as a reflection of God's character, this law is written into the very fabric of creation. God's revealing the law to Israel is in itself an act of grace, so they might know him and his ways in this world. Yet there is also a problem. The people have an inclination toward rebellion, and they are simply unable to keep the requirements of the law. But God is committed to relationship with these people—so what happens? God in his wisdom had written into the law an older and more primal "incantation," which foresaw the problem and made provision: a perfect person could act as substitute for the imperfect, dying in their place. Since no such person would be found, God would have to do it himself by offering his own Son. God's Son would accomplish for his creatures what they could not accomplish for themselves.

This does well in capturing Deuteronomy's view of law and grace. On the one hand, the book sees the law as something good and even attainable:

> Now what I am commanding you today is not
> too difficult for you or beyond your reach. It
> is not up in heaven, so that you have to ask,
> "Who will ascend into heaven to get it and
> proclaim it to us so we may obey it?" Nor is it
> beyond the sea, so that you have to ask, "Who
> will cross the sea to get it and proclaim it to
> us so we may obey it?" No, the word is very
> near you; it is in your mouth and in your
> heart so you may obey it. (Deut 30:11-14).

The passage contrasts how most of us understand the law—as something foreign and outdated—and instead characterizes it as a good and fitting gift from the hand of God. In this way, Deuteronomy portrays the law like Deep Magic in Narnia.

Yet on the other hand, Deuteronomy looks down the corridors of time and foresees that further measures will be needed:

> When I have brought them into the land
> flowing with milk and honey, the land I
> promised on oath to their ancestors, and
> when they eat their fill and thrive, they will
> turn to other gods and worship them, reject-
> ing me and breaking my covenant. ... I know
> what they are disposed to do, even before I
> bring them into the land I promised them on
> oath. (31:20-21)

Moses holds out little hope that the people will be able to obey the law. Yet, curiously, he also speaks of a time when the people will return to the Lord, and the Lord will return them from exile:

> When you and your children return to the
> LORD your God and obey him with all your
> heart and with all your soul according to
> everything I command you today, then the
> LORD your God will restore your fortunes
> and have compassion on you and gather you
> again from all the nations where he scat-
> tered you. Even if you have been banished
> to the most distant land under the heavens,
> from there the LORD your God will gather
> you and bring you back. (30:2-4)

There is, therefore, a significant question raised by Moses' words: how can he hold out little hope of the people's obe-dience yet foresee a future for them as God's people?

The answer comes in a fleeting comment, which, like a bolt from the blue, strikes and then is gone again:

> The LORD your God will circumcise your
> hearts and the hearts of your descendants,
> so that you may love him with all your heart
> and with all your soul, and live. (30:6)

The answer, we learn, is that the Lord *himself* will accomplish the change of heart. He will accomplish for Israel what they could not accomplish for themselves. And through this act, their hearts will be turned toward their covenant Lord.

We do not learn from Deuteronomy how such a feat will be accomplished, only that it will be accomplished. But other books in the Old Testament do go on to develop the idea. The prophet Jeremiah reveals that the Lord will make a new covenant with his people, a covenant whose main difference is not substance but location: it will still be based on law, but law written on human hearts rather than stone tablets (Jer 31:33). In this way, the natural desire of God's people would be obedience to God and his ways. But how exactly would the law be written on human hearts in the first place?

The prophet Ezekiel speaks to this question, foreseeing a time in the future when God would put his spirit in people:

> I will cleanse you from all your impuri-
> ties and from all your idols. I will give you
> a new heart and put a new spirit in you; I
> will remove from you your heart of stone
> and give you a heart of flesh. And I will put
> my Spirit in you and move you to follow my
> decrees and be careful to keep my laws. Then

> ... you will be my people, and I will be your
> God. I will save you from all your unclean-
> ness. (Ezek 36:25–29)

God's indwelling spirit would write his ways upon people's hearts, empowering them to obey the law.

But there was just one more problem: how would the people be cleansed from all their impurities, as Ezekiel said, so that God's Spirit could dwell within them? The prophet Isaiah reveals the answer to this when he speaks of the suffering servant, who, though righteous, would suffer and die on behalf of the sinful:

> But he was pierced for our transgressions,
>   he was crushed for our iniquities;
> the punishment that brought us peace was
>   on him,
>   and by his wounds we are healed. (53:5)

It is no accident that the language here sounds sacrificial, for the passage envisions the man as a sacrificial lamb. While such an idea is familiar to us today, it would have been earthshaking in Isaiah's day. It would have put into people's minds a singular question: who is this man that will take away our sin?

In Jesus of Nazareth we finally behold the man—a carpenter's son, born to a humble family in rural Palestine. This man would go on to live a righteous life and, in so doing, upset the religious authorities, who would hand him over to be crucified. Yet just as Isaiah predicted, this very act of killing a righteous person would accomplish God's work. That is why Christ, before dying, could say truly, "It is finished" (John 19:30). In this way, he would forever bind the people to their covenant Lord by writing God's law on their heart. Like Aslan's self-sacrifice on the Stone Table, Christ's crucifixion revealed that behind Deep Magic was a deeper magic: "that when a willing victim who had committed no treachery was killed in a traitor's stead, the Table would crack and Death itself would start working backward."

Knowing God through the New Covenant

God's grace is the deeper magic, the silver thread that holds together the old and new covenants. What this means, in turn, is that grace is the enduring refuge of God's people and a defining quality of God's character. It also means that if we are to know God truly, we will know him through grace. But how do we do this?

The mistake many of us make is in thinking grace is passive. It's as if we can acknowledge the existence of grace and be done. But grace is something that we partake of, not merely observe, and we do this through two activities: pursuing complete devotion to God and receiving his mercy.

In listening to some speak of grace, you might think it erases the need to pursue God in the first place. But nothing could be further from the truth. Grace itself presumes a context of need. We cannot even comprehend grace until we've tried and failed to embody Christ perfectly in all circumstances, everywhere, at all times. A person sitting in the paddling pool cannot hope to appreciate life guards at the beach. But a man who's been pulled out to sea by a riptide and, having swum and swum unto exhaustion, lay face down in the water waiting for his end, only to have a lifeguard pull him to safety and revive him—that man will have a great appreciation for lifeguards. So it is with grace: we can only recognize it from a perspective of need.

Building on this, we must also learn to receive grace. More often than not, we hold God's grace at arm's length because we're not willing to acknowledge our own need for it. I'm thinking of the tendency to generalize our failings, conveyed through phrases like "I'm not perfect" or "we all make mistakes." The problem with this is that it has the appearance of acknowledging guilt without the substance, for it requires no reflection or ownership of personal wrongdoing. It simply speaks what we already know about humanity generally.

Can you imagine if we behaved like this at the doctor's office? Let's say I know my arm is broken and that the doctor can fix it, but when he asks what ails me I speak in generalities: "Well, you know, we all have problems" or "I've had my share of pain in life." It would be an utter waste of time. The only way for the doctor to heal me is to identify, as closely as possible, the nature of the injury, so that he can do his work.

The point, of course, is not to saddle ourselves with more guilt. Precisely the opposite is true. We already carry within us guilt about things we've done or left undone, so to acknowledge our failings is simply to bring to the surface what already exists beneath it. In so doing, we discover it is like exposing a submerged iceberg to sunlight, which melts away whatever ice comes to the surface.

God's grace is like the sunlight. It is always shining and so is always available, but it can only do its work when sin is brought to the surface. Bringing sin into the light is not hard in theory, but it requires great courage. It requires confessing our sins before God and people and repenting. Yet when we are able to do so, we come to know God through perhaps *the* defining aspect of his character— grace. God's grace is the great hope of Deuteronomy, and God's grace is still the enduring hope of the church.

SUGGESTED READING

☐ Isaiah 52:13–53:12

☐ 1 Corinthians 15:1–28

Reflection

Do you find the idea of Deep and Deeper Magic helpful in understanding the old and new covenants? Why or why not?

_____

_____

_____

When Aslan says that "death itself would start working backward," what does that mean? How might the above passages flesh out the biblical picture of this?

_____

_____

_____

_____

What are some practical ways in which you might make room for God's grace in your daily life?

_____

_____

_____

_____

CONCLUDING THOUGHTS

Deuteronomy is a timeless text, calling out to each new generation to come and know God better. The Ghost of Christmas Present, from Dickens's *A Christmas Carol*, serves as a good analogy, for he calls out to Scrooge, "Come in and know me better, man!" The ghost then shows Scrooge images of what has been and, depending on Scrooge's action, what might be. In so doing, he emphasizes the fleeting nature of the present and the importance of making good decisions *now*. Similarly, Deuteronomy calls people to come and know God better, reflects on his past goodness, and envisions a future with him. Its call is an urgent one, expressed in the defining exhortation of the book: "Now choose life" (Deut 30:19).

Yet Deuteronomy does more than invite people to come and know God; it also provides the *means* for knowing God. We looked at five such ways: memory, worship, law, covenant, and grace. Deuteronomy 1–4 sets the stage by portraying Israel's journey with Yahweh as an ongoing journey into which each new generation of believers must enter through memory. As Christians, we enter this journey through the Lord's Supper, remembering Christ's death and resurrection. Deuteronomy 5–11 shows worship as the way in which we journey with the one true God rather than an imposter of our own making.

Moving from worship to righteous living, Deuteronomy 12–26 demonstrates that the law still has relevance for us today as a sanctifying force. By observing rituals, such as the Lord's Supper, we come to embody certain dispositions, and dispositions, in turn, are what shape our living. Above all, gratefulness is what characterizes Deuteronomy and what we learn through practicing the Lord's Supper. Deuteronomy 27–34 rounds out the book by portraying the ongoing means of knowing God: covenant relationship. Covenant, we said, is unique in that it provides a safe environment—a sanctuary of trust—in which we can grow in our knowledge of God and ourselves. As with marriage, the key is a stable environment in which we're free to be ourselves without fear of abandonment.

The final means of knowing God was grace. While people do not often associate grace with Deuteronomy, grace is written into the very DNA of the book. The central call of the book is for people to love God with an all-consuming passion and reckless abandon, a task that the people will fail at. Yet Moses holds out hope, for as he looks down the corridors of time he sees a solution: God himself will accomplish for his people what they could not do for themselves. The Old Testament's whispers and glimpses of what this might mean take form, finally, in Jesus of Nazareth: "a willing victim … killed in a traitor's stead."[20] The enduring message, then, is that to know God truly is to know him through grace, shown ultimately in the person of Jesus Christ.

We have come full circle, and it is fitting to finish with the lyrics that began this book and that summarize Deuteronomy:

Oh to grace how great a debtor,
Daily I'm constrained to be
Let thy goodness like a fetter
Bind my wandering heart to thee

May this be our own prayer as we seek to know God better.

SUGGESTED READING

☐ Reread Deuteronomy from start to finish.

Reflection

What were two things that surprised you about the book of Deuteronomy?

_____

_____

_____

_____

What were two of the most impactful things for you?

_____

_____

_____

_____

Finally, what are two things that you would like to study
further in Deuteronomy?

_____

_____

_____

_____

RECOMMENDED READING

For good and readable commentaries on Deuteronomy, I recommend two to begin with: Peter C. Craigie, *The Book of Deuteronomy* (The New International Commentary on the Old Testament; Grand Rapids: Eerdmans, 1976) and Christopher J. H. Wright, *Deuteronomy* (New International Biblical Commentary; Peabody, MA: Hendrickson, 1996). Craigie's work, especially, looks at issues of historical background, while Wright is strong on ethics and mission.

For a longer and more detailed though equally readable commentary, I suggest Daniel I. Block, *Deuteronomy* (The NIV Application Commentary; Grand Rapids: Zondervan, 2012). To my mind, this is the best single-volume commentary available in English at present.

As for special studies, I recommend two: J. Gary Millar, *Now Choose Life: Theology and Ethics in Deuteronomy* (Leicester, UK: Apollos, 1998) and Richard S. Hess, *Israelite Religions: An Archaeological and Biblical Survey* (Grand Rapids: Baker, 2007). Millar has been helpful in highlighting certain aspects of Deuteronomy's theology, such as its emphasis on journey, and this book makes his ideas accessible to a wider audience. Hess's work is helpful in a different way. Deuteronomy is a book long embroiled in historical questions, which further reading will reveal. The volume by Hess is valuable because it locates the biblical texts, including Deuteronomy, alongside the most important archaeological discoveries and frames the texts within their historical context. While it may be demanding for some, for those looking to consider the historical issues, Hess's work is a very good resource.

NOTES

1. Peter Craigie, *The Book of Deuteronomy* (NICOT; Grand Rapids: Eerdmans, 1976), 79–83.

2. John Leland, *Why Kerouac Matters* (New York: Viking, 2007), 17.

3. J. G. McConville and J. G. Millar, *Time and Place in Deuteronomy* (Sheffield: Sheffield Academic Press, 1994).

4. G. K. Beale, *We Become What We Worship* (Downers Grove: InterVarsity Press, 2008), 16.

5. Daniel Block, *Deuteronomy* (NIVAC; Grand Rapids: Zondervan, 2012), 160.

6. A. W. Tozer, *The Knowledge of the Holy* (New York: HarperCollins, 1961), 1.

7. Tozer, *Knowledge*, 4.

8. C. S. Lewis, *A Grief Observed* (London: Faber & Faber, 1961), 66.

9. For full instruction on this practice, see Kevin O'Brien, *The Ignatian Adventure* (Chicago: Loyola Press, 2011).

10. See Sandra Richter, "The Place of the Name in Deuteronomy," *Vetus Testamentum* 57 (2007): 342–66.

11. J. G. McConville, *Deuteronomy* (AOTC; Downers Grove: InterVarsity Press, 2002), 220.

12. John Piper, *Desiring God: Meditations of a Christian Hedonist*, revised edition (Colorado Springs: Multnomah Books, 2003), 18.

13. Smedes, "Controlling the Unpredictable: The Power of Promising," in *Christianity Today*, January 21, 1983, 16, 17.

14. Smedes, "Controlling the Unpredictable," 18.

15. Smedes, "Controlling the Unpredictable," 18.

16. Smedes, "Controlling the Unpredictable," 18.

17. For more on this, see Richard Hess, *Israelite Religions* (Grand Rapids: Baker Academic, 2007), 216–21.

18. C. S. Lewis, *The Lion, the Witch, and the Wardrobe* (New York: HarperTrophy, 1950), 147–82.

19. David Lyle Jeffrey, ed., *A Dictionary of Biblical Tradition in English Literature* (Grand Rapids: Eerdmans, 1992).

20. Lewis, *Lion, Witch, Wardrobe*, 160.

LEXHAM PRESS

TRANSFORMATIVE WORD SERIES

An engaging, thematic exploration of the Bible, offering refreshingly unique insights within each book of the Bible.

Learn more at LexhamPress.com/Transformative

Revealing the Heart of
Prayer
The Gospel of Luke

CRAIG BARTHOLOMEW

2 CORINTHIANS

CUTTING TIES WITH DARKNESS

JOHN D. BARRY

TOG

THE BOOK OF ESTHER

God Behind the Scenes

WAYNE BARKHUIZEN

When You Want to YELL AT GOD

The Book of Job
Craig Bartholomew

SS
ONE
REVELATION

W Y. EMERSON